The Little Book on Digital Marketing

The Little Book on Digital Marketing

SEO Part 1
On-Page Optimization

JOSEPH STEVENSON

Published in the United States by
Joseph Stevenson Publishing.
Josephstevenson.com/little-book/

ISBN 978-1947215016

Printed in the United States of America

First Edition

For my kids,

Joshua, Eliza, Eric, and Katie

Don't forget to always work on your inside before working on your outside.

Contents

01

Introduction

Why I Write This Book and How It Can Help

"It's not about money or connections - it's the willingness to outwork and outlearn everyone... And if it fails, you learn from what happened and do a better job next time."

— Mark Cuban

Why

The Purpose of This Book

If you haven't already, I would suggest you pick up a copy of the first book in *The Little Book on Digital Marketing* series entitled "Keyword Research."

This book is a follow up on how to properly optimize a website with the most profitable keywords.

It is important to know how to find and target the right keywords before learning on-page optimization so that you don't waste time creating content that highlights the wrong things.

Assuming you have already picked it up, or that you already know keyword research, I'll move on to the point of this book.

Make it Great

As I mentioned in my last book, I am often emailed and called for advice on digital marketing by competitors, students, potential clients, and others. Usually, I get calls because a website I was marketing received higher visibility, creating a mad rush to find out my secret sauce for success.

I don't believe in any secret ingredients, but instead, I focus on doing the right things over a long period of time, which inevitably leads to greater results.

Achieving great results starts with a great product or service. If you have a mediocre business, then your results will be mediocre. More than half of the successes of SEO-enabled websites have to do with the quality of the site itself and the underlying business model. Those who focus too much on driving traffic without focusing on the user experience will never get anywhere with SEO.

The purpose of this book is to help you make "it" great – no matter what the "it" is on your website. Whether you sell widgets or services, I hope this book will show you the proper way to optimize your site for the maximum effect and ability to rank in major search engines.

Additionally, this book, the prior volumes, and the ones to come, will focus on the aspects of digital marketing that will produce the best long-term results. Each on its own should be a good resource, but together they make a blueprint for your online success.

Things May Change Over Time

Since digital marketing changes constantly I would assume at some point this book would have outdated material. With that in mind, I will attempt to share general theory on how a specific skill or principle works, instead of specifics about a tool or website.

I will use websites as examples and case studies but my hope is to teach skills and not give a direct reference to a tool that may not be around in ten years.

While writing this book, backlinks seem to be the most influential piece of a website that determines its ranking. Within a few years it may shift to something totally different.

I won't speculate on where things are going but instead, will focus on sound principles that should stand the test of time and teach you enough to adjust your website as SEO rules change.

You May Disagree with Me

Digital marketing is a broad topic and interpreted differently by a variety of experts. There are so many techniques that it would be impossible to write a guide and have it accepted by everyone.

With that in mind feel free to disagree with me. I would love feedback! You can participate in online chapter discussions through my blog at https://josephstevenson.com. Go to the learning area and click on the chapter you are currently studying. Please leave your comments, corrections, feedback, or additions in the comments section.

Even if we disagree I will gladly publish your opinion as long as it is a professional response free from spam or vulgarity. I'll also publish your emails to littlebook@josephstevenson.com.

How

The Process

Much like the last book, I have broken each chapter into sections to help facilitate learning.

Each chapter should be read in order since we start with simple concepts and move on to more complex ones later in the book.

Chapter Structure

Each chapter is divided into six parts encompassing:

- How
- Why
- Case Studies
- Goals and Actions
- End of Chapter Challenges, and
- Citations.

Why: This section will cover why this topic is important and how it can benefit you. It will contain examples and stories of successes in using this specific principle. Think of it as my sales pitch on whatever the chapter is on.

How: Once I have "sold" you on the idea, my goal is to teach you how to apply it to your own situation. I will give examples of how I used the technique and other resources so you can do the same.

Case Study: This section will contain a real-life example of a company or companies that have applied the principle with great results.

Things to Ponder: In this section, I put the most relevant points to focus on. I suggest you re-read this book occasionally to brush up on the skills you've learned. The Things to Ponder section will give you the best overview and thought points.

End of Chapter Challenge: I believe we learn best by practicing, so each chapter will end with a challenge. Even if you feel like you know everything about a specific subject, complete the challenge. It will help you retain what you learned.

Citations: I've listed all cited resources from the chapter here in case you prefer to wait until the end to look up the sources. I will also post the citations for each chapter on the blog for easier navigation.

One Final Note

This book will focus solely on on-page optimization and how to get your website in the most optimal place to rank online. My hope is that this book will help you get your website from good to great not only for optimization, but structure, speed and overall user experience.

I intend this book to help business owners, marketing managers, students, and anyone interested in digital marketing or optimization.

There are so many online resources meant to give you eighty or ninety percent of the truth with the rest available for purchase in a subscription or package.

It can be frustrating when you're trying to learn a new skill to have some of the information withheld for a price. I hope that I can convey the full one hundred percent of each principle so you won't feel ripped off or left with a feeling like you'll need more information at the end of a chapter.

If you do have additional questions, please go to josephstevenson.com and click on the learn area. From there the chapter discussions will allow for additional insight.

Although each chapter is set up to be read through in the order it was written, feel free to skip around and write in the margins. After all, this is your book as much as it is mine. Diving in will be the best way for you to learn a new skill. Let's get going!

02

Meta Tags

"Some people exert more energy on less important things; some people exert less energy on less important things."

— Ernest Agyemang Yeboah, *Distinctive Footprints of Life: Where Are You Heading Towards?*

Why

Doing the Most Important Things First

Meta tags [1] are the most important part of on-page optimization. Meta tags consist of titles, descriptions, and other page-defining information.

The reason they are the most important, is because they are the describers of your website pages. When you do a Google search, the blue text at the top is your title meta tag, and the grey text below the blue link is your description tag.

Years ago, there were keyword tags but those became obsolete when too many people stuffed them full of keywords to try and game the search engines.

Meta tag descriptors are what search engines crawl to determine what your page is about. Meta tags also provide users with the first impression of your website.

Having incorrect or poorly formatted meta tags can cause a bad user experience leading them to possibly bounce from your site.

Getting the Right Mindset

Before worrying about the benefits of meta tags and how they can help you with SEO, make sure you are in the right mindset on how meta tags work.

Meta tags are designed to describe a page. They do not rank a page in search engines.

Most sites get in trouble for bad SEO for trying to "trick" Google and other search engines into ranking them higher for keywords their page is not about.

If you worry about describing your content first before ranking it, you will avoid any possible issues with ranking loss from bad page meta tags.

Different Types of Meta Tags

When it comes to rankings, there are a lot of [2] meta tags out there, with some more important than others. Here are some of the more popular meta tags and their purposes for web pages:

Title: The page title is the first meta tag that search engines see. The title shouldn't be more than 60 characters [3] to avoid having the search engine only show parts of it.

Additionally, it should include the main topic of the page and the site name. For example, my site is josephstevenson.com and I do SEO Consulting as one service. An optimal title tag that includes my business name and page topic could be, "SEO Consulting Services | Joseph Stevenson."

Description: The description is the summary of your webpage and should contain about three or four sentences total. Additionally, it shouldn't have more than 160 characters [4] for the same reason the title tag shouldn't have more than 60 characters. The meta tag should be about the page and shouldn't have repeated sentences. Using my example from before on SEO Consulting this would be an acceptable meta description tag:

"Joseph Stevenson is an SEO Consultant based out of Las Vegas NV. He has provided his services for over 17 years in the web and SEO industry."

You may notice that I used the word "SEO" twice in the meta description. It is OK to use targeted keywords more than once, but make sure you have compelling copy that isn't full of spam.

Otherwise, you will risk having issues with possible rank loss over keyword stuffing.

Keywords: Keywords aren't used by any major search engines anymore due to abuse by website owners. The idea behind the keyword meta tag was to tell search engines what that page should rank for. Pretty nice back in the day, but once everyone caught on you can imagine how that was no longer helpful to search engines.

Robots: Search engines crawl your site with what they call spiders or robots. The robots meta tag tells them whether you want to be crawled or not. Some sites that are private or only want certain sections of their content indexed would block the robots or tell search engines not to crawl their sites. On the flip side, any site that needs organic traffic as a part of their strategy would want this meta tag to allow crawlers.

Revisit-After: This is a piggy back meta tag that goes hand in hand with the robots meta tag. It is used to tell search engines how frequently to crawl the site. There are other tools like Google Webmaster Tools [5] that make this an obsolete tag as well.

Other Less-Used Meta Tags

Along with the major meta tags there are also some minor ones that aren't as important. The reason I say less important is because I haven't found a big impact on SEO if these aren't used. It's important that I note them but most sites will auto-add them for you.

Copyright: Explains how the text and images are protected on a page.

Googlebot: Tells Google's crawler what to do when on your site. This can be handled through Webmaster Tools now.

Language: This sets the preferred language of the site.

Reply-to: For bloggers who want requests sent to a specific email address.

Web_author: Although not used anymore by Google, a year or so ago you would see pictures of authors next to content in the search results. While this has disappeared, you can still have author information in the meta tag for any site-crawler looking for it.

HTTP-equiv: This is for setting cookies and describing other functions of the page. It's a bit technical and is usually handled by plugins that perform the actual functions.

Now that we have covered the major meta tags, lets move on to how we implement them into our sites to improve rankings in search engines.

How

The Process of Meta-Tag Implementation

As I mentioned before, the meta tag is what should describe your page. It is the blue and grey text in search engine results that describe what you're clicking on.

You could learn how to find and target keywords with the right volume and difficulty level by using principles taught in the Keyword Research book from *The Little Book on Digital Marketing* [6].

Once you know what keyword you want to target you should create content around that keyword in a non-spam way.

Example of spam content: I do SEO as an SEO Consultant and I am the best SEO person that does SEO in the world.

Example of non-spam content: I am an SEO consultant offering services to businesses looking for help with online marketing.

When you find a keyword, you want one you can create content around that describes and uses it as the topic of the page. We'll go more into that in the text area of this book but make sure when you are creating your meta tags they also aren't spam or keyword stuffed.

That is bar far the best way to get on Google's bad side.

There are multiple ways to implement meta tags into your webpage. It's important to make sure each page has them. If you set up a Google Webmaster Tools account you can get your site crawled and view any errors for pages that are missing meta tags.

The two main ways to create meta tags: Automatic and manual.

Automatic

Automatic meta tag creation is, as its name implies, automatic. Search engines such as Google will crawl your page and use the content to populate your query results.

The most common content automatically used for meta tags are your H1 tags and the first lines of content in the paragraph tags. Meta tags can also be pulled from tag managers like Google Tag Manager. [7]

Not having a meta title or description is considered pretty bad on-page SEO, but the worst case is if you don't include these in your code. Although, Google can still pick up on what your page is about just by reading your content.

This is another good reason to build good content around targeted keywords, just in case Google can't see your meta tags and ranks you for the content being read.

I wouldn't recommend using the automatic method since you will be completely at the mercy of what the search engines want to index. At the same time don't lose too much sleep if you don't have proper meta tags because search engines are smart enough now to auto index what your content is about.

Manual

The second way to get your meta tags indexed by Google is the manual way. Manual, meaning you manually tell the search engines what your title and description should be.

The easiest way to do this is to use a plugin or theme that will allow you to customize your title and meta descriptions. If using Wordpress, my favorite plugin is Yoast [8] for on-page optimization.

With Yoast installed, you can view the page you are editing through a dashboard that will walk you through your on-page setup.

Once you have specified what keyword you are targeting in the dashboard, you can edit the title and meta tags. If you have too few or too many keywords in the meta tags, Yoast will tell you and keep you out of trouble.

If you are a beginner or an experienced digital marketer, I would suggest using a tool like this to help you fill out your meta tags manually.

The benefit of the manual process is that you have full control of the user's first impressions of your site. You decide the site title and description before anyone clicks your link.

The cons of course are that you may be biased and not completely on-point with what your title and description are. If you create a title tag that isn't descriptive enough, you risk a lower ranking due to irrelevance.

Google will have its own opinion of what your page is about and what your authority is on the page's subject. Manually creating meta tags is important, but make sure you are targeting what your page is actually about, not just what you want to rank for in Google.

As long as you keep your pages relevant to their descriptive tags, you won't have any issues with lower rankings from on-page screw-ups.

Case Study

Henderson SEO

For years, our company ranked number one for everything related to "Las Vegas SEO." It was our bread and butter and I hadn't really considered targeting other keywords.

The city I actually live in is Henderson, which is a suburb of Las Vegas much like Summerlin or North Las Vegas.

So, I decided to try an experiment to see if I could rank for the search term "Henderson SEO." The search volume was pretty small for this keyword but I wanted to add authority by being number one for both Henderson and Las Vegas.

The first step was to write completely new SEO content related to Henderson. I made sure it was customized with no resemblance or copying from my Las Vegas SEO page.

After creating the content, I put up a second location page that had a similar design structure to my Las Vegas page. I made sure that the images and other media were focused on Henderson and not Las Vegas.

My title description read:

"Henderson SEO or Search Engine Optimization | Joseph Stevenson"

My description read:

"Henderson SEO for individuals looking for great SEO and web design at terrific costs contact our Henderson SEO Joseph Stevenson."

After publishing the page, I made sure any reference to my Las Vegas page didn't include Henderson - and vice versa for the Henderson page.

After a couple of weeks, the only off-site SEO I published was a quick PR update announcing that we service Henderson now.

The results were nothing less than extraordinary. Firstly, we ended up ranking number one almost immediately. We also were able to get solid PR for ranking well for multiple cities.

I mainly attribute the success to the strength of the site in the Southern Nevada area, along with the well structured on-page content including the meta tags.

When publishing this book, we still rank well for both keywords and we haven't adjusted our meta tags for quite a while. This hopefully proves the point that going for quality content that is relevant will always trump any other scheme to rank well.

Things to Ponder

1. What is your main product or service?

2. If you read the pages on your website, how closely do they represent your product or service?

3. If you found your website on Google and read the blue title tag and grey description, how closely does it represent your product or service?

4. Of the pages on your site, which ones do you think users should see first? Which pages would you rather they see last?

5. Are there any pages that don't belong on your site? Are there any title or description tags that describe content no longer relevant to your business?

6. How do your meta tags stack up against competitors? Are their meta tags more or less relevant than yours?

End of Chapter Challenge

This end of chapter challenge will focus on proper creation of meta tags that describe your page content.

Don't worry about how much traffic your page will get related to the keywords you target.

(If you haven't already, check out the Keyword Research section in the *Little Book on Digital Marketing* which covers that in depth.)

If you're using Wordpress, download and install the Yoast SEO plugin. If you are using a build it yourself site like Wix [9] or Squarespace [10] the meta tag builders should be built into the settings of each page.

Once the tool is installed, review the content of your page by reading through it.

After your review, what keyword(s) would best

describe the page? Write them below:

Keyword(s) ________________________________

Next, add the keyword(s) to your target keyword section in the Yoast plugin under editor settings.

You should see a grade come up automatically for how your page relates to the keyword(s).

Without editing your actual content, go to your title and description area and change it to say:

[keyword] - Your Site Title

Then change your description to summarize the page using your keyword at least once. For instance:

Joseph Stevenson is a [Las Vegas SEO] consultant and loves to fish, surf and play with his kids.

After changing your title and meta descriptions check your score again. Now, if you have any negative scoring, assume it's related to your content and not your meta titles.

How well did you stack up? If your content has no keywords at all you should probably re-write it.

If it contains some keywords but not enough, then that's probably a good place to start. If you have too many keywords, you need to learn not to over spam site content and be a little more original in your writing.

Don't worry too much if your content receives a low score at first, the next section will show you how to properly create content that will match your meta tags in both accuracy and authority.

Citations

[1] Meta Tags, W3schools.com, https://www.w3schools.com/tags/tag_meta.asp

[2] The Meaning of all the Different Meta Tags and How to use Them, metatags.org, http://www.metatags.org/all_metatags

[3] Meta Title Length, MOZ https://moz.com/learn/seo/title-tag

[4] Meta Description Length, MOZ https://moz.com/learn/seo/meta-description

[5] Google Webmaster Tools, http://google.com/webmasters

[6] The Little Book on Digital Marketing (Keyword Research) josephstevenson.com/little-book/

[7] Dynamically Added Meta Data, https://www.simoahava.com/seo/dynamically-added-meta-data-indexed-google-crawlers/

[8] Yoast Wordpress Plugin, https://wordpress.org/plugins/wordpress-seo/

[9] Wix, Personal Website Builder, http://wix.com

[10] Squarespace, Personal Website Builder, http://squarespace.com

Online Resources

Online resources for this chapter can be found at:

https://josephstevenson.com/little-book-seo-part-1-on-page-ch2/

Links to citations, discussions and submission of additional resources by readers are available for each chapter.

To be notified of future books in the Little Book on Digital Marketing Series please email littlebook@josephstevenson.com or visit our website at http://josephstevenson.com/little-book/ and enter your email in the form provided.

Text

"Give them quality.
That's the best kind of advertising."

— Milton Hershey

Why

Viewing Your Website Through the Eyes of Google

Have you ever wondered what your website looks like to a search engine spider?

When we see a website we see logos, text, images, colors, ads, animations, forms and much more. We of course are humans with eyes ears and emotions. We interpret what we see in positive, negative or indifferent ways.

Search bots on the other hand do not interpret things like we do because obviously they are pre-programmed to do the same thing every time they read through a page online.

Often when there is an update to a website, the owners will see a decrease in rankings and immediately exclaim, "Google hates me!" The reality though, is that the crawler was adjusted to more accurately read and interpret the page. That leads to the updated websites getting a few less thumbs up than others.

People are rarely targeted directly by search

engines. Instead, their rankings are directly related to how well their content is laid out.

Meta tags are the first point of reference for a search bot. Like what we discussed in the last chapter, your meta tags will tell Google what your page is about.

Once in a while Google and the other search engines will automatically index your meta titles and descriptions, even if they were manually set. In their Search Console [1] Google explains that rendering of a web page happens in different ways and how they index your content is up to them. Here is what Google says from their own website on the subject:

> Rendering is another process Google uses to understand how your web pages look and behave for your users on various browsers and devices. Similar to how a browser displays a webpage, Google retrieves your URL and executes the code file for that page (usually HTML and JavaScript). Google then crawls all the resources in the main code file references (usually images files, style sheets files and other JavaScript files) to ultimately paint the visual appearance of your page and get a better understanding of your content.

In a nutshell, don't assume you have full control over how search engines view or index your site.

With this in mind it is important to know how the search engines are viewing it so you can create content in a way that will best index your site for your targeted keywords.

Text That Can Stand on its Own

As I mentioned before, how we view a web page is different from a computer spider's view of our webpage.

Here are a few examples of how a search engine "sees" your website:

Image: When a search engine crawls a page where you see an image the search engine sees <img src="imageurl" />. We will go into image optimization later, but it is important to know how search engines see things before knowing how to optimize them.

Video: Videos are similar and usually display in an iframe with something like this: <iframe src="videosrc"></iframe>

Links: Where you see a hyperlink to another page search engines see <a href="linksrc">Go to this page</a>.

Do you see any commonalities between how each html code is displayed on a site?

If not, don't worry, that's why I wrote this book.

A search bot reads your entire site as text. From images to videos, and colors to tags, it is all text to Google.

When you are reading this book, you see black letters on a cream colored page. If a search engine was reading it the code would tell it the background is #f7f7f7 and the text color is #000000.

It can seem a little overwhelming at first when you realize how much you have to spell out for search engines, but it also gives you a lot of power over how your content is read and indexed.

The goal when writing text for your site should be to create content that can stand on its own without a lot of descriptive tags or meta keyword suggestions.

A good example would be Wikipedia and their many pages of content. If you look up bicycle on Wikipedia [2] you will see that the page has mostly text, hyperlinks to related content, and a few images.

If you were to remove the images and hyperlinks the page itself would still be very much about bicycles.

This is what I mean when I suggest creating stand-alone content. You'll want to make sure that whatever point your content is trying to get across is contained in the page text.

All too often I see the main topics of websites written over the top of an image that is placed on the page. It is possible to rank based on a good alt and title tag of the image, but not as good as plain text. Overall, text will usually trump tagged media almost every time, so keep that in mind when adding content to your website.

Topic First Sales Second

A good rule of thumb is to worry about the content topic first and sales second.

Bad content can always be spotted a mile away with it's "Won't last long!" or "special offer for only 24 hours!" text smeared all over the page.

If a website contains only sales material, it had better be a landing page for pay-per-click (PPC) ads.

Otherwise you're going to be competing with the millions of websites that are improperly optimized for "Won't last long!" So, you will never rank for whatever product or service you're trying to sell.

Let me give you an example. If you sell garden hoses good copy would be something like:

> Green Lake garden hoses for sale.
> We have the highest density, no kink, garden hoses on the planet. We use only synthetic rubbers and green technology for making our product.
>
> See what some of our customers have said about their purchases.

Notice that in the content we mention garden hoses but we also talk about what we make them out of and how high quality they are. We then insert testimonials from clients, which will probably contain more text about garden hoses.

With a page like this we are covering our content base by focusing solely on garden hoses. We may have minor text somewhere that shows where you can go to purchase them, but that is not our primary topic.

By focusing on our product first and sales second, we have a much better chance to rank for our fake company name of Green Lake Garden Hoses along with garden hose-related keywords than if we had focused solely on selling garden hoses without any good copy.

In the next section, I'll cover how to properly create content that search engine's love and the process you should go through every time you are creating content.

Once you have a solid process down for creating content around your target keywords it should become much more natural to write text that can be indexed and ranked by search engines. Creating natural content is the quickest way to add value and rank your website higher.

How

The Process of Good Content Creation

Having a process for content creation is important not only for website consistency but also to help you stick with to the subject of your page.

The following paragraphs demonstrate my process for creating content. This isn't the only way to do it, but it works for me. Take it, mold it and create your own process for content creation.

Within the process I will list the major things you need to consider while creating content that is search engine friendly and good for ranking higher.

Step 1: What is the Main Page Topic?

I first determine what the page is about. This goes beyond the keyword, instead focusing on what I want the users experience to be. For instance, if I'm targeting people looking for SEO Consultants in Las Vegas, what should the page show? Should it be informational or directed towards services offered?

Once I have defined what the page topic is, I usually write it down on a whiteboard or somewhere I can see it so my mind stays on topic.

Step 2: Define the main headings.

Once I know my main topic I will pick at least five main content headings. If I am targeting people looking for SEO Consultants in Las Vegas and I want to show them educational information, my topics would probably look like this:

- What we do as consultants
- Average cost for SEO consulting
- Testimonials from consulting customers
- What to consider when starting SEO consulting
- Contact information for consulting services

Each one of my points focuses on my main topic, which makes it easier to write content in different areas that all focus on the same area.

If you notice, each subheading focuses on SEO consulting, which makes that an easy target for the content under each heading.

Step 3: Write main heading content backwards.

I prefer to write the content backwards on a page. Some people find this odd, but it allows me to separate out each section without requiring any of them to depend on each other. I prefer stand-alone content, so this is a style that works for me. If you want each section to build off of the last, this would probably not be a good approach. Again, mold it to your own style.

Write at least 200 words for each section below the headings. This will allow you to have around 1,000 words on the page for Google to crawl through. The minimum suggested word count is 300 [3] words per page. Going with 1,000 will give you plenty for indexing.

Step 4: Add content to web page and grade it.
After you have constructed the content and added it together with headings, it is time to publish and grade.

If you are using Wordpress, install the Yoast [4] SEO plugin and enter your target keyword in the meta field.

Based on how well you stuck to your topic, your

grade will either be green, orange, or red. The grader will crawl the content based on the exact number of keywords contained in the text that related to your targeted keyword. It isn't a perfect way of doing things but it definitely gets the job done.

Step 5: Match meta tags to your content.
As we discussed in our last chapter, you will want to make sure your meta tags include the main topics contained in the text. Both your meta tags and text are the biggest determiners of on-page quality rankings, which is why I address both of them in the first two chapters of the book.

If you are using Yoast, you'll notice solid meta tags and content will help the majority of your grades to stay green. The same is true with many of the other on-page graders out there.

By focusing on the content first you are removing the doubt search engines have when crawling unrelated site text about page topics.

The Main Takeaway

The main thing to take away from this chapter is to focus on your topic first, sales second.

Don't worry about whether people will buy from your content. You can always adjust your copy later to convert more. If you never rank in the first place, you'll never be able to test different copy out, anyway for ROI.

Play it safe and focus on quality first; the sales will come later.

Case Study

Urologists Vs. Urology

One of the best clients we have ever worked with was a urologist targeting a mid-sized city. I say "best" because whether they were happy or upset with the results they were always professional and pleasant to deal with.

One of the main keywords they wanted to target was urology in the town where they were located. We were able to create content that helped them rank relatively easily for urology-focused keywords. Mission accomplished. Or so we thought.

What we found over time was that the urologist keywords were not doing well at all. In fact, all of the urology keywords had very strong rankings, but every single urologist keyword was not on the first page of Google.

After doing some research we found that every page on their site had good content, but it was all focused-on urology not urologists. The content had targeted urology so well with meta tags supporting the content, that the related term of urologist didn't stand a chance. It was almost as foreign to the site as baseball gloves.

We did rank usually on the second page of Google for urologist keywords since it was in the same realm, but we all know the second page of Google is the best place to hide a dead body -- keyword rankings there don't mean a whole lot.

The Solution

Our plan was to intermingle the keywords related to urologists with the urology keywords so that the pages could rank equal on both. My concern was that we might lose in rankings on the urology side of things, but hopefully, not much.

After making the changes we did notice a slight drop in our urology keyword phrases but our urologist phrases jumped right onto the first page.

At that point we only needed to do some off-page SEO (covered in the next book) which pushed their rankings steadily into the top three.

The lesson learned was that content targeting keywords works, but sometimes too well. We needed to make sure we focused on the topic just a little more broadly to achieve the rankings we were hoping for.

Things to Ponder

1. What are the main topics on your website? Are these topics broken out by page?

2. How much content is on each page of your website? Is the content well written or very sales oriented?

3. Out of the content written right now, how well would it stack up in the grading process?

4. Do the meta tags auto generated from your content describe the point you are trying to get

across?

5. Do you enjoy reading the content yourself? Is it exciting, boring, neutral, or factual? Is it something you are proud to have on your website?

6. What content isn't on your site that should be there? How would that content benefit your readers or users?

End of Chapter Challenge

In this end of chapter challenge, I am going to mix things up a bit with two different exercises.

Exercise 1

First go to Google and type in a search term you feel best describes your business. If you do this right you should see some competitors show up.

If you see your own site, then good job! Now pick a high-ranking competitor and go visit their site.

When you're on their page, right click and then click on the "view page source" link. From here a new tab or window should open with the source code of the page.

This source code is what Google reads. Go line by line and see how much of it makes any sense to you. How much text do you see that focuses on the keyword you searched for in Google? How much is hard to understand like images or videos? JavaScript is especially fun to read for non-programmers.

Do this for a few competitors so you can see what Google is seeing when they crawl websites.

Usually the highest-ranking sites have the best on-page structure, so as you go down the list the source code related to the targeted keywords tends to get progressively worse.

Exercise 2

After looking through some competitor's source code, it's time to put together some content.

Go to your website, or if you don't have a website, use a Word document.

Determine the five main points your business is about online. These should be the five main things you want other people to see if they come to your website. Remember that these are people who know nothing about your business so you have to be very detailed about what you do.

For my business, I want people to see these main pages:

SEO Services
Consulting Services
Learn SEO
Podcast
Contact Us

These are my targets because I focus on educating and providing high quality services to my clients. All of my links are related to either services or free educational offerings.

Once you have determined your main focus points, pick one to create content on.

Create another five that focus on the main targeted keyword for the page. (See the prior exercise.) Once you have them listed, write a minimum of 200 words under each of the five headings.

If you have an existing website and are comfortable with the content, put the page up, fill in the meta tags, and add the content exactly as you wrote it.

Additionally, check your current keyword rankings in search engines *before* you put the content up and then again once per week for the next month after you add new content. Notate any changes in ranking below:

Target Keyword: ___________________________

Ranking Before Content Change: ___________

Ranking After 1 Week New Content: ________

Ranking After 2 Week New Content: ________

Ranking After 3 Week New Content: ________

Ranking After 4 Week New Content: ________

If you don't have a website, set up a free blog on blogger [5] and do the same exercise.

How did the results pan out? Did you see an increase in rankings for your keyword based solely on the content you created? Did other keywords decrease?

Overall Results:

____

____

____

____

____

____

____

____

Citations

[1] Google Search Console, https://support.google.com/webmasters/answer/6065802?hl=en&ref_topic=6065797

[2] Bicycle, Wikipedia, https://en.wikipedia.org/wiki/Bicycle

[3] Optimal Word Count, SEO Book,

http://www.seobook.com/archives/001986.shtml

[4] Yoast SEO Plugin, http://yoast.com

[5] Blogger, Free Blogging Platform, https://www.blogger.com

Online Resources

Online resources for this chapter can be found at:

https://josephstevenson.com/little-book-seo-part-1-on-page-ch3/

Links to citations, discussions and submission of additional resources by readers are available for each chapter.

To be notified of future books in the *Little Book on Digital Marketing Series* please email littlebook@josephstevenson.com or visit our website at http://josephstevenson.com/little-book/ and enter your email in the form provided.

04

Links and Style

"No man will make a great leader who wants to do it all himself or get all the credit for doing it."

– Andrew Carnegie

Why

The Differences

This chapter will focus on internal and external website links and content text styles. These may seem like very trivial on-page subjects but there is actually a lot that should be taken into account when creating content with links and stylized text.

Google and other search engines learn a lot about websites based on the internal and external linking behaviors and the bolded, underlined or italicized text.

Some of the most important text on the page is the bolded text naturally specified as the main header or h1 header [1]. This is widely accepted as the most important tell of the page's subject.

In this chapter, we will break out links and stylized text and talk about the importance of both. Then I will show you how to properly implement both into your webpage for maximum on-page SEO benefit.

Let's start with internal links.

Internal Links

Internal links are hyperlinks to other pages within your website. When search engines crawl your page, they read through the text and every time a link is found the crawler will follow that link to that page and crawl it as well.

Most sites have built in sitemaps that tell search engines about all the pages included on their site. Even with this map, internal links are important to help search engines understand what is most important on your site [2].

Imagine you have a website that is geared towards selling bicycles. Let's assume you have 10 different bicycle models to sell and a blog with tips and tricks in the cycling industry.

Properly using internal links will allow higher authority pages on your site to surpass the rankings of less popular pages. An example would be if you have a Huffy Bike page that gets a lot of hits per month.

You could create a piece of content on the Huffy Page that says something like:

"If you are interested in our Huffy Bikes you will also probably love our Trek Bikes."

After you create the content you would want to link the text "Trek Bikes" over to the Trek Bikes page. What this does is create a reference inside your site and adds one more internal vote to the Trek Bike page that you should rank for that keyword.

Sites with proper internal links will have a general structure that is followed consistently. Each page should reference other pages on the site, which shares their authority and spreads the SEO love around. We'll talk more about this in the How section.

External Links

External links are also important to your on-page SEO efforts but also have the potential to do a lot of harm if not done carefully.

The links themselves are very powerful when it comes to SEO and should be handled with care.

Internal links allow a lot of leeway if you mess them up, and external links can drop your rankings quick if you use them improperly.

Google's purpose is to bring the most relevant content to users. In order for them to do this, they have to put what they view as the most helpful and informative content first.

Websites that are only self-promoting with no external links are about as good as a tabloid making news up out of thin air.

On the other hand, websites that have lots of references and proof of their facts from other websites will build more trust and rank higher.

Every page on your site should reference at least one other page and if possible a page that is not a part of your website. I will go into details on how to decide what pages to link to so you won't hurt your rankings or inadvertently help your competition.

Style

The style of your text is what tells search engines what is the most important content or description of text.

Humans can visually see what is important in

text by how large it is, whether it's bold or italicized, and a myriad of other styling options that show importance.

Since crawlers aren't able to detect the size or styling of a font, we have to highlight what's important when creating the content.

Take this book as an example. This section has Internal Links, External Links and Style as the main sections. Those are the most important pieces I wanted to talk about.

You probably knew this because you saw that the text was bolded and centered. If you had been a computer, they would have just been other words on the page. Hence explanations are necessary.

Links and Style Together

I hope you will view links and font styles together as equally important. Some digital marketers pick something as a favorite and lean heavily on it during optimization.

I would suggest checking out Wikipedia pages [3] to see how many internal links; external links and style changes there are in the text. Seeing the volume of styling in terms of text importance for search engines can dramatically change how you perform your on-page SEO for links and styles.

How

Using Links Properly

Links are meant only for reference or navigation purposes. When you are adding links to your website whether they are internal or external, you should always keep the purpose of your content at the forefront of your mind.

Using links in the proper way will add more quality to your website than adding them just because you can.

When linking to content there are a few rules of thumb that you should keep in mind.

Do and No Follow: When you add links to your site you have the option to add do or no follow to the rel element. This tells search engines whether they should crawl that link [4]. It also tells them if you should pass any SEO value your page has through to the linked page. This is true for internal or external links.

You can decide on whether to pass value pretty easily these days. If the content is positive and not a crummy site, feel free to do follow to them.

Google takes into account how you link to other sites. A big issue is accidental transfer of SEO value through improper backlinks and dofollow links.

New or Same Window: When a link is clicked you can have it open a new window or stay in the same window. Generally, if you are staying on one site you should have it in the same window. If you're linking to another site make the user experience continues in the same window. If you are linking to a reference or verification source that is meant to be temporarily open, use a new tab.

Anchor Text: What the link says tells search engines a lot about what that page is about. If you have a contact page linked from your home page, you could make the text say anything from "contact us" to "give us a call!"

When search engines crawl links they take into account the name of the link in determining how to rank the page.

Use proper meta tags that explain the page in a simple way so that the links will pass on authority in relevant areas.

No So Fun Fact: If you were to use a do follow link to your competitor with an anchor text that was your main keyword, you could potentially pass the majority of your rankings on to them. The lesson. Don't link to a competitor ever; even if you are just referencing them.

These three uses of backlinks are probably the most important ones to consider when creating links both internally and externally on your website.

There are others, but if you stick with these guidelines, you will be covering most of your bases.

Proper Use of Text Styling

Much like text backlinks, there are also different ways to style non-clickable content.

As I mentioned before, you have to tell search engines what font is large, small, bolded, italicized or underlined. All of these styling options give signals to Google about what the page is supposed to convey.

Listed below are some of the major tags to wrap your content in, and what they mean to search engines:

H1: The h1 tag tells search engines that this is the most important topic of the page. If you are trying to rank for "Dog Bath Services" your h1 tag should probably say that [5].

H2 - H6: The "H" in h tags means heading. H1 is the most important and h2 - h6, all tell search engines the other main points of the page. You will want to add them in order so that like subheadings in a book, they can tell Google what the most important topics are on that page.

Bold: The bold tag <b>, is used to tell search engines what's important within a paragraph. This is helpful for keyword targeting or topic suggestions.

Italic: This tag slants your text, which suggests to search engines that it is an explanation or quote. This is helpful when citing other sources and you want to call it out from your original content.

Underlined: Much like bold but not as important. The underline is another way to say text is important but doesn't carry as much weight as the bold tag.

Cross-Out: Use this tag if you want to show corrections in the text but still need to leave the old content as reference. This helps search engines see changes in your content and text that is no longer relevant.

Highlight: Some text may be highlighted different colors. This may not have much affect on search rankings but it is helpful for user experience in seeing what is important on the page.

Tying Them Together

The purpose of styling text and linking to other pages and resources, is all about user experience.

When creating content, keep in mind the user who will be reading it. What is most helpful to them? What will keep them on your site longer?

What will help them navigate around your site in a simpler way?

Keeping the user experience in the front of your mind with keyword integration as a close second will be the best thing you can do for your on-page SEO.

Sites that have good content and styling tend to keep users longer and improve the overall experience. This in turn signals Google -- and the quality of your site and your rankings will naturally increase.

Proper linking throughout your site with highlights on important keywords are also subtle ways to tell search engines how your content should be indexed and read.

Remember quality first, optimization second, and you will end up with much better results than your competitors.

Case Study

Careerfield

One of the first websites I ever built was a job board called Careerfield. This was a basic site that indexed jobs from around the web for easy searching by users.

In the beginning, I would index the job title and description. Once in my database I could show them on a webpage using the same job title and description I had indexed.

Although this wasn't a bad idea for navigation and page identifying, it was a horrible idea for SEO.

Search engines picking up the jobs on my site saw them as duplicate content since they had been on other job boards first. My rankings never got up much past the 2nd or 3rd page leaving me with very little traffic.

Once I realized my on-page text and headings were identical to other competitors, I changed my strategy and made my on-page text and links to be more unique.

Instead of just showing the job title as my `h1`, I added the city, state, and category of the job.

In the description, I highlighted and bolded important text and phrases. I would also add descriptive text unique to each job. Additionally, I styled these differently so each would be seen as a resource.

The results were nothing short of miraculous. Over the course of a few months our traffic went up to more than 30,000 daily hits. Our ad revenue quadrupled, and users were staying on the site longer.

Besides adjusting the content to be unique and sending it back out to search engines, we did nothing else to see those results. It was a pretty powerful lesson about on-page changes.

Things to Ponder

1. What are the current `h1` tags on your website? Do they accurately describe what the page is about?

2. What other headings, if any, are on your

website? Are they properly labeled h2 - h6?

3. What text on your site is bolded or underlined? What text is styled differently on your pages? Are they highlighting important areas of your content?

4. What links are in your content from page to page? Are the internal links relevant to other pieces of content or just navigational?

5. What external links are taking people away from your site? Using principles from the Keyword Research volume, are the sites being linked to higher or lower quality than your site?

End of Chapter Challenge

Site audits are regularly performed for clients by professional SEOs. Some of the audits include on-page checks.

This end of chapter challenge is meant to teach you how to do a basic on-page SEO audit of your website.

First write down the keyword your home

page is supposed to be ranking for:

Keyword: ______________________________

Next go to your home page without logging in to your site. Right click and view the source code. Once the source code window comes up click CTRL F or Command F if you are on an Apple computer.

Type in the search box `h1` and the `h1` tag should highlight in the code. Write down what the `h1` tag is:

H1 ______________________________

Do a similar search and write the first tags that come up:

<b> ______________________________

<strong> ______________________________

<u> ______________________________

<a href ______________________________

<p> ______________________________

<i> ____

<h2> ______________________________________

<h3> ______________________________________

<h4> ______________________________________

<h5> ______________________________________

<h6> ______________________________________

Now review your answers and see how many of the tags describe or have to do with your main keyword topic.

You may be surprised at how different or similar they are. Remember that search engines only know what they read on your page, so the more accurate your text and links are, the more accurately you will be indexed in search engines.

Citations

[1] Search Engine Journal, Importance of H1 Tags, https://www.searchenginejournal.com/in-2014-how-important-is-an-h1-tag-for-seo/

[2] MOZ, Internal Links, https://moz.com/learn/seo/internal-link

[3] Wikipedia, http://wikipedia.org

[4] Wordstream, Follow Links Vs. No Follow Links: Should You Care?, http://www.wordstream.com/blog/ws/2013/07/24/follow-nofollow-links

[5] W3schools.com, HTML <h1> to <h6> tags, https://www.w3schools.com/tags/tag_hn.asp

Online Resources

Online resources for this chapter can be found at:

https://josephstevenson.com/little-book-seo-part-1-on-page-ch4/

Links to citations, discussions and submission of

additional resources by readers are available for each chapter.

To be notified of future books in the *Little Book on Digital Marketing Series* please email littlebook@josephstevenson.com or visit our website at http://josephstevenson.com/little-book/ and enter your email in the form provided.

05

Images

"We are what we repeatedly do.
Excellence, then, is not an act, but a habit."

- Aristotle

Why

The Importance of Images

Web designers and developers often overlook image optimization. That's why the majority of images online are indexed incorrectly due to poor optimization.

This leads to less traffic for the website owner, and less relevant searches for image users.

If you are reading this book with your eyes you may not have thought about what those who can't see do for books or other media. Maybe you have.

Either way, someone who is visually impaired can't see text, let alone an image on your website. Search engines have been able to crawl and index your content to make it accessible for the visually impaired but images are a different story.

Besides trying to make your content the most valuable you can for all users, properly optimizing images and other media will help your rankings just based on overall user experience.

Google rewards content that is optimized for all

users [1], as that will put the most accurate content in front of everyone, not just those who have good eyesight.

Besides the obvious reasons for descriptive and properly optimized images, there are other reasons to properly optimize your media.

Better Index: Images that have the proper tags, names, and sizes tend to rank better in search engines and other image indexes.

Easier Caching: Usually a size issue but images that have been properly optimized tend to cache better than others that take up too much bandwidth causing loading issues for some devices.

Accessible on Multiple Devices: Properly optimized images load better on all devices including mobile and tablet vs. non-optimized images that take too long.

Plain Text Vs. Images

Some websites have almost no images. If you go to sites like craigslist.org [2] you won't see any images on any of the pages except for postings.

This allows the site to load very very fast for most users.

On the flip-side, sites like imgur.com [3] are mostly made of of images and despite the lack of text, still tend to rank well in search engines.

The question then is whether images are important to optimization or if a site can get along fine with only text.

Brian Dean from Backlinko [4] sums it up nicely I think in his article about on-page SEO:

> Another reason to optimize your images for SEO: it gives search engines another clue of what your page is about...which can help it rank in organic search.
>
> When Google sees images with alt text “blue widgets” and “green widgets” it tells them: “this page is about widgets.”

I am pro-image usage for sites. While I think you can get by without them, it is one extra piece of unique content that tells search engines what your page is about. If you really don’t want to use them, at least put an author bio at the bottom of your page with your image in it.

How

It's A Pretty Quick Process

So, optimizing images is actually not that big of a deal. You need to know a few things and follow a process, but once you do it a few times it becomes a habit.

I will list the steps I follow when optimizing images for website inclusion. As always, if I miss anything please add it to the blog at https://josephstevenson.com/little-book/ and I will post it online.

I will list some of the most used steps but there will be others I may not include. Since this book is about SEO, I will try to stick with the things that will benefit your site for SEO not just image optimization.

Image Width/Height. If you have ever used the Google Page Speed insights tool [5] most likely you have noticed the optimization error that comes up pretty often. A lot of webmasters think this is related to image size only, but in fact it also has to do with the actual width and height of the image.

The idea is that if you have a space on the page

that is only 600px wide but an image that is 700px wide, the image will be too large for the area. Play it safe and create images that fit in the space you've reserved for them on the web page.

If you aren't sure how to do this add something like the Page Ruler [6] tool to your browser and then select the area your image will go in. You should be able to see the size of the image area.

If you aren't sure how to re-size your image you will probably want to do a Google search incorporating whatever program you are using.

Each major image display program or editor has a resize option making it pretty simple to do.

Image File Size: OK, so once you have the right width and height, it's time to work on file size.

Google loves lossless compressed images since they are much quicker to load and store. I prefer to use sites like Compressor.io [7] but any compression engine will do. Once you have the image sized correctly for width and file size you are ready to upload.

Tools like Google's site speed checker will tell you exactly how much memory you'll save by compressing the image. If you do it correctly the error should go away completely, signaling an image size that is optimized correctly.

File Name: File names are actually pretty important. They tell Google what your image is.

Many cameras or stock photos use alphanumeric strings to label images. Although this is helpful in identifying unique database images, it is pretty horrible for search engines to identify what the image is about.

File names can contain letters, numbers, dashes or underlines. As long as you know what type of image you have, renaming it to something search friendly is as easy as right clicking it when it is on your computer and then clicking the rename button.

If you have a jpg or png image you will most likely see something like:

"298rhsdjhfd.jpg" as an image name. This is a great example of an image that isn't identifying itself to search engines.

If your image is of a man and woman holding hands consider renaming the image to be something like:

Man-woman-holding-hands.jpg or man-woman-with-hands-together.jpg. The keyword selection up to you, but try to focus on keywords that support the overall page topic. If the image itself has nothing to do with the page topic or keywords, that is a good signal to find a different image.

Title Tag: The image title tag tells search engines what the image is. It's just like the name of the image as we previously discussed, but you will add it as you would read it. The title tag is added to the image code like the following example:

<img src="/imagesrc.png" title="Man and Woman Holding Hands" />

Having a title tag that supports the keyword and file name is a great way to describe the image to search engines.

Alt Tag: The alt tag is a descriptive tag for images that don't load or that can't be seen by visually impaired users. If your title tag is "Man and Woman Holding Hands" that could be considered enough to tell a visually impaired person about the image.

However, the alt tag should be a descriptor that tells us as much about the image as possible, kind of like the paragraph below the title in a story.

You may want to consider alt tags that are helpful in every sense such as:

Man, and woman in a park holding hands while sitting on a bench.

This paints a clearer picture and will put your site leaps and bounds in front of competitors who have boring or no alt tags at all.

Captions: These are used for both visual and indexing purposes. Some of the most popular reasons for using a caption is to give credit for the image to the creator.

Captions can also be used to talk about the image like an alt tag but the proper way is for credit or reference. Captions are usually placed below an image.

Using our previous example, you may have the image with a man and woman sitting on a park bench and the caption below would read, "man and woman sitting on park bench courtesy of John Doe Photography."

By using all of these options to optimize your image, you should now be ready to upload it to your website for use in pages, posts, galleries, etc.

When you upload the image, you can test all of the attributes through tools like Yoast [8] or Google Page Speed insights as mentioned before.

Properly optimized images will not only help your user experience, but also give you the opportunity for more traffic from image searches online.

Case Study

Free Desktop Wallpaper

One of the first websites I built was a free desktop wallpaper index. The concept was simple; store wallpapers that users could download free of charge for use as backgrounds on their computers.

Initially when I built the site I didn't think much about image optimization, but instead focused on the text optimization around the image hoping that would help with indexing.

Not surprisingly, I didn't have a lot of luck the first couple of months with my project, largely because of the poorly optimized images.

After doing some research, I realized I needed to make some changes. I ended up changing all of the image title tags. At that point, I was just testing, so I didn't do any further research but instead just changed the title tags.

By adding keywords to each image in the title tag area I found that 90% of my images jumped up in image searches to the top 3 results, which in turn drove thousands of new visitors to my site.

Changing the title tag alone had helped these images rank so well above competitors that I didn't even mess with other optimization methods.

I later abandoned the project due to the cost of licensing the images and a lack of monetization of the site. But the lesson remained with me and I still use it continually to properly optimize websites images.

Things to Ponder

1. What images do you use on your website to describe the content?

2. Do the images properly describe what you are talking about, or are they stock photos that just look pretty?

3. Of your images, how many are full size that take a while to load, versus smaller images that fit the viewport area?

4. Are the images necessary to the design of the page or added purely for SEO purposes? Are there better images that would describe your content?

5. Are any of the existing images already optimized? Are you able to find them by doing basic searches in Google Image search?

End of Chapter Challenge

In this challenge, I want you to practice optimizing images and uploading them on to you site.

To start, pick a blog post that is already published with no images. If you have added images to all of your posts, then just edit any post.

This should hopefully give you less worry about messing up your site, since blog posts tend to get less traffic than main pages.

First, check the max size of the area that the image will be in. Use the ruler or other tool mentioned earlier. Usually the max size will be what the image size is on desktop computers. Mobile devices should size the image down automatically if you have it inserted correctly.

Add the size in the provided below for easy recollection, while we go through this challenge.

Image Viewing Area Size ____________________

Next select the image and in an image editor

make sure the width and height does not exceed the area size on the page. If it is, re-save the image as a smaller size to fit the viewport area.

Next add the keyword your page is targeting:

Target Keyword: ______________________________

Since you should be optimizing your image to support the page topic and keyword, write down the information that should be used in the different image tags:

File Name: ______________________________

Title Tag: ______________________________

Alt Tag: ______________________________

Once you have added all the necessary tags and sizing, upload the image into your site.

Last of all, use Google Page Speed insights to check for errors on your page. If you have a properly optimized image you shouldn't have any errors show up.

You should also consider using a grading tool like

Yoast to tell you if the image properly targets the keyword for the page.

Citations

[1] Google Image Publishing Guidelines, https://support.google.com/webmasters/answer/114016?hl=en

[2] Craigslist, http://craigslist.org

[3] Imgur, http://imgur.com

[4] Backlinko, On Page SEO, by Brian Dean http://backlinko.com/on-page-seo

[5] Google Page Speed Insights, https://developers.google.com/speed/pagespeed/insights/

[6] Google Chrome Page Ruler, https://chrome.google.com/webstore/detail/page-ruler/jlpkojjdgbllmedoapgfodplfhcbnbpn?hl=en

[7] Compressor.io, Compress and optimize your images, https://compressor.io/

[8] Yoast Optimization Plugin, http://yoast.com

Online Resources

Online resources for this chapter can be found at:

https://josephstevenson.com/little-book-seo-part-1-on-page-ch5/

Links to citations, discussions and submission of additional resources by readers are available for each chapter.

To be notified of future books in the *Little Book on Digital Marketing Series* email littlebook@josephstevenson.com or visit our website at http://josephstevenson.com/little-book/ and enter your email in the form provided.

06

Videos/Music

"It's alive! It's alive!"

- Frankenstein, 1931

Why

How Media can Help

Do you know what the second largest search engine is in the world? As of today in 2017 it is Youtube [1] coming in a close second to Google [2].

Many people are using Youtube for entertainment, education, work, testimonials, and more. If I hadn't mentioned the name of the site, though, it could have qualified as any other large site.

Just because a site has content for entertainment, education, or work, etc., doesn't mean the medium in which the content is delivered necessarily matters.

Why then are images and videos helpful in presenting content and for on-page optimization?

Enriching the User Experience

SEO in and of itself can make the user experience on your site so good that you get high rankings from search engines based on quality alone. The idea is that if you create great content, others will link and talk about you, which in turn will increase your rankings.

Although some sites do well with just text as their media (like Craigslist) [3], normally you will need some type of rich video or image content to improve the user experience. We already talked about images, but not videos, and music, which have a different method for optimization.

When online content was first accessible, there wasn't a lot of media available due to Internet capabilities and the slow load time. Most websites would have background colors instead of background images, and any of these were usually very small so they would load as quickly as possible.

Videos were basically non-existent due to the inability to embed them, but also because they would have crashed any sites or browsers trying to load them.

Oh, how far we've come in such a short time!

Back then, even with precautions, many large sites would take time to load such as Myspace [4] page load speed was still a major issue and sites with too much media would crash.

Now that the Internet and website hosts have better connections it isn't usually an issue to have images peppered throughout websites. If anything, for your website to be taken seriously, it's expected have a lot of media.

Why Videos and Music Matter

Text on a website can tell a story, but images and video can show it. According to Liraz Margalit Ph.D., from *Psychology Today* [5], watching a video and reading an article activate separate cognitive functions. Liraz says:

> "Whether it's YouTube, Vine or integrated content, video has quickly become one of the most impactful ways to speak to an audience. According to a recent study by Usurv, if you want visitors to your site to share and interact with your content, delivering it via video is the best way to go. Consumers are 39 percent more likely to share content if it's delivered via video, and 36 percent more likely to comment, and 56 percent more likely to give that video a coveted "like."

To put it in another perspective, think about a recent online purchase you made. Most people will look for online product reviews to see what other people's experiences have been.

I recently made such a purchase for a dolly I needed to move a pretty large object. I was worried about the weight capabilities etc., so I started doing my research.

There were a lot of options out there, but the one I settled on had a video of people using the product and showing different objects being moved.

The competitors had great reviews but no videos or other media to show me how great it was.

When I received the product, it worked perfectly which reinforced my desire to see this type of content in the future before I make purchases online.

I know there will be some bad experiences for users and it won't always work perfectly for everyone who creates this type of content, but the point is that videos and music help to tell a story much better than only text and images.

How

Proper Embedding

You can either upload music and video to your website, or third-party websites, that you embed on your site.

I'll quickly go through the pros and cons of both, but my personal preference for SEO is to always use a third-party site like YouTube and then embed the video into your site.

Pros Versus Cons

Most website owners who self-host videos and music do so for the control it offers. Generally, there is a fear of media being compromised or owned by a third party, which is why they won't put their video or music anywhere they don't have full control.

You definitely have more control of your content if it is only uploaded on your website and nowhere else. The biggest con though, is that usually private servers don't have the ability to cache the video content in a way that makes it quick loading for new users.

In recent years third party sites like YouTube have given more content control to the creators by allowing privacy to be set up in ways that protect content.

Nowadays you can upload videos and make them private so only users with a password can view them. This makes it very easy for you to upload a video and embed it on your site with security settings that make it only viewable from certain pages.

Additionally, self-hosted videos provide less SEO value than third party videos that can show up as their own search results based on your tagging and keyword practices.

Optimizing videos and music works the same whether you're using your own server or a third party site. To keep things simple, I will go through the main steps for optimizing videos for your site by using third party sites.

If you want to use your own site to host the media, follow the same steps, but when you embed the video you will need to use an internal html code to show the video versus the embed code provided by sites like YouTube or Vimeo [6]. If you aren't sure how to do it just check with your developer who should be able to upload and show your video on your site within a few minutes.

Optimizing Your Media

Music and videos are very similar formats, which is why I combined them for this chapter. The steps to optimize them are also similar and should work regardless of if your media is video or music.

I mentioned YouTube and Vimeo already for video and there are also great music sharing sites as well like Sound cloud [7], which allow you to upload your tracks for the public.

Step 1 Pre-Upload: Before uploading your video to any third-party site you will need to make sure your file is properly optimized. Do this by compressing the file much like you did for images. This will improve the load speed.

You will also want to follow similar steps as with images by naming the file with the targeted keyword, like "how-to-change-oil.mp4." Since you are uploading a file make sure to check all the settings for any internal tagging so you can add target keywords to all applicable settings.

Step 2 Upload: Most sites now have a quick drag and drop feature for uploading, making it very simple. Additionally, the fields to fill out while the file uploads are pretty self-explanatory. Make sure to fill out all fields using your target keyword including the title, description, tags, keywords, categories, etc.

Once you have added the content to the fields, go through all the settings for hearing impaired users, like closed captions. Most images, videos and music that have proper closed caption encoding will rank better because the user experience is going to be better.

Step 3 Playlists and Categories: Once your file is uploaded you will be able to add it to playlists and social media sites. Sharing is caring, and the more you share the better off your content will be. Use the social sharing buttons to add the video to all your profiles including Twitter [8], Facebook [9], and Google+ [10].

Crawlers like Google inspect new content on these sites, which index your content higher.

Step 4 Embed: Once you have finished the above three steps, you will want to copy the embed code and place it on your site where you want the video to air.

Most embed codes will give the video a pixel width, which can mess up mobile sites. Change the width="" to have 100% versus a pixel width. Then adjust the height to whatever pixel looks best.

Last, have your developer cache the JavaScript resources used to load the video or music. This will get rid of any Google Page Speed Insights [11] errors from the video loading and taking up space.

Case Study

Orthodontics

A long-time client wanted to start putting content on YouTube related to orthodontics and braces.

They have good, unique content and they wanted to make sure they were offering value. After talking through best practices for uploads, they created a video around taking care of braces.

After optimizing their settings and uploading the video, they shared through social media and then left it alone.

The results were pretty astounding. Within a year they had hit over one million views organically and as of today they have more than 1.8 million views of their video. Mind you, this is a video hosted only on YouTube. They don't have this video embedded anywhere on their website or elsewhere. They also haven't done any SEO or promotion.

Their only strategy was to created good content, tag it properly, upload, share, and keep an eye on it.

The organic work handled the rest for them with minimal effort.

I don't think their success was based only on their proper SEO practices they used but instead was a mix of quality content, proper uploading and keyword selection.

At the time, there wasn't very much competition for "how to take care of your braces," so they filled a need for people searching.

The point is that unlike many of the "success" stories you hear but can never achieve online, this client stuck with the basics and after uploading over 50 videos, had one hit a vein, and take off like crazy.

Things to Ponder

1. What videos or music will best explain your product?

2. Where do you host these videos now? Is the platform you use providing good or bad user experience?

3. How optimized are your videos? Are they uploaded with the default name of the video or was it optimized to target specific searches?

4. What is the video intended to do? Educate, inspire, humor, entertain etc.? Does your site content match up with the goal of the video? Does the video help promote what is on your site, or would it confuse a visitor if it was posted on its own?

5. Is your video optimized like your images for

hearing or visually impaired users?

End of Chapter Challenge

This end of chapter challenge will be easy for some and difficult for others. If you are already familiar with making videos and music to upload online you can probably skip this section.

For those who haven't done it before, don't get discouraged. If you have any difficulties go back and re-read the How section of this chapter.

First, select or create a video about a product or service you offer. Identify the keyword or topic you want to address in the video:

Keyword: ______________________________

You can start with a video from your phone. Once the video is created, upload it to your desktop so you can begin optimizing it. Once you have it optimized follow the steps below with your file before uploading it to YouTube.

1.Rename file to match the keyword you selected (Example: dog-food-ingredients.mp4).

Video Name: ______________________________

2. Compress video using an online video compressor service.

File Size Before Compression: _____________

File Size After Compression: ______________

Next upload the video to your YouTube channel. If you don't have a channel yet, sign in to YouTube with your Gmail account and follow the prompts.

Once you're on your channel, select the video upload link and drag your file into the uploader.

3. Add all applicable fields with keyword related content.

Video Title: ______________________________

Video Description: ___________________________

____

____

____

Video Categories: _________________________

Video Tags: ______________________________

Once you've uploaded the video, share it to your social media platforms and if available, embed the video on your site for on-page SEO value.

To see how relevant your video is to searches based on your optimization, track video views over the next month:

Week 1 Video Views ______________________

Week 2 Video Views ______________________

Week 3 Video Views ______________________

Week 4 Video Views ______________________

Citations

[1] Youtube, https://youtube.com/

[2] Google, https://google.com/

[3] Craigslist, https://craigslist.org/

[4] Myspace, https://myspace.com/

[5] Psychology Today, Video vs Text: The Brain Perspective https://www.psychologytoday.com/blog/behind-online-behavior/201505/video-vs-text-the-brain-perspective/

[6] Vimeo, Video Sharing Site, https://vimeo.com/

[7] Soundcloud, Music Sharing Site, https://soundcloud.com

[8] Twitter, https://twitter.com

[9] Facebook, https://facebook.com

[10] Google +, https://google.com/plus/

[11] Google Page Speed Insights, https://developers.google.com/speed/pagespeed/insights/

Online Resources

Online resources for this chapter can be found at:

https://josephstevenson.com/little-book-seo-part-1-on-page-ch6/

Links to citations, discussions and submission of additional resources by readers are available for each chapter.

To be notified of future books in the *Little Book on Digital Marketing Series* please email littlebook@josephstevenson.com or visit our website at http://josephstevenson.com/little-book/ and enter your email in the form provided.

07

Plugins/Tools

"A tool is but the extension of a man's hand, and a machine is but a complex tool. And he that invents a machine augments the power of a man and the well-being of mankind."

- Henry Ward Beecher

Why

Importance of Tools

The plugins and tools on a website are as essential as the content they display. Gone are the days of hand coding content through html templates or line items.

Plugins and tools help us display content in a way that is more meaningful without causing us hours of coding and learning new tactics that we may only use once.

Previous to the age of Content Management Systems [1], tools or plugins didn't exist for many website owners.

If you wanted to have a slideshow of images, you would need to hand code each slide into the page and then write your own JavaScript to play the slides. I remember, because I've built quite a few sliders from scratch before plugins were invented.

With the introduction of plugins, we were able to take a difficult task and simplify it with a piece of code to do the work for us. With this wonderful new thing, though, came a few downsides.

What to Watch Out For

Developers from all over the world write Plugins. There is no real vetting or checking of their work to make sure it is clean code that's free of bugs or security issues.

Even though the pros of having a pre-built plugin run portions of your site are great, there are some major cons that warrant an entire chapter in this book on how to optimize plugins for SEO. Here are just a few.

Speed: Plugins or tools can range from one to thousands of files added to your site. Depending on the developer's style the code could be well written or a complete mess.

Page speed is a huge contributor to your on-page optimization. With that in mind, it is important that you don't add plugins or files that are so bloated, it slows your entire process down.

Security: Many plugins require access to your database. If you install a plugin that isn't secure, hackers could use it to access your website and database. Once in, they can wreak havoc.

Non-Compatibility: Some plugins don't play nicely with others and although they offer something you need, it may not be worth having other plugins or site options not working. Unfortunately, there isn't a great way to check compatibility without installing and running the plugin to see if anything breaks.

Are the Pros Really Worth It?

The short answer is -- yes. There are a lot of very good plugins out there that don't require massive site bandwidth, but will save you in by-hand coding.

You'll find that often the plugin developers built what you needed better than you would have been able to. All of the cons, although valid, shouldn't outweigh the pros.

How

Optimizing Plugins for SEO

Knowing the risks and issues with plugins and tools, it's now time to learn how to optimize plugins for SEO.

There is a lot that goes into on-page optimization

for SEO but some of the major points are keywords, content, page speed, and security.

Plugin optimization addresses all of these on-page points, making it one of the more important but often overlooked SEO practices.

It's vital to take time to check and optimize each plugin or website tool if you hope to have a clean on-site experience. Ignoring them will slow your site down and give your competitors (who are willing to put the time in) the edge they need.

Most of the remaining How points of this chapter will be very technical so I will try to put them in lay terms so you can request help from your developer, if needed. This isn't to say you can't do them yourself, but I would recommend getting help since some of the updates could harm your site if done incorrectly.

Rendering

The majority of websites online have the error I am going to go over. Fixing these issues can greatly improve your site speed.

Using Google Page Speed Insights [2], type in the

home page URL for your site.

Once you have added the URL, you will probably see an error that says:

> Eliminate render-blocking JavaScript and CSS in above the fold content. None of the above-the-fold content on your page could be rendered without waiting for the following resources to load. Try to defer or asynchronously load blocking resources, or inline the critical portions of those resources directly in the HTML.

What does this mean?

Render blocking JavaScript [3] and CSS is computer language, or code, used by plugins or tools that load plugin data. Since the plugin needs these files to operate, removing them is not an option.

Have your developer look at the different code that needs to be optimized and have them add in the async attribute to each one.

If this does not clear up the issue, have them copy the code directly into the page as inline content.

This will remove the need to load any external file and should remove the error.

BEWARE: Plugin developers periodically update some code and inline insertion of the code, which could disrupt the user experience.

Caching

JavaScript resources that need to be loaded for plugins often do not cache for more than 15 minutes. The issue this causes is that every time your page is loaded it re-grabs the JavaScript and causes loading time to be longer than it should be.

Search engines don't like this and so caching all cacheable resources is a must.

Caching [4] is basically taking a picture of a file and storing it so you won't have to re-load the entire file over and over again. The easiest way to look at it would be to think of looking at a page that has text on it. Each word if stored as text would need to be added to the file. If, however, you take a picture of all the words, you only need to load the picture.

The up side is you can load content quicker, but

the downside is you have to remember to clear your cache when content is updated, otherwise the old content will show versus the new.

Your developer should be able to log in to your server and set the cache settings to be as strong or as light as you would like them. Having a good cache set up is important, since it will reduce page speed loading for users, improving their experience, and keeping you in good graces with Google.

If caching methods do not work with a specific plugin, I would recommend uninstalling it and finding another. The less plugins you have on a website the faster it will load, but beware of bloating your site with too much inline code since that could cause other issues.

Quick Wrap Up

Since plugins can be very difficult even for developers to optimize, try to think through the importance of each one before using it.

Some sites rely heavily on plugins so that employees who are not tech savvy can make even the most difficult content edits.

Other developer-run sites have very little if no plugins, which helps keep the running site faster.

A best practice would be to have trusted friends or peers review your site and give you feedback on what functions influence them, and which don't. Often something we see as non-negotiable is just something we are biased towards because of the time or effort we have already put in.

Case Study

Wedding Chapel

Usually my case studies have happy endings but unfortunately this one does not. It does serve as a good lesson though, which is why I wanted to include it.

Having our primary office in Las Vegas gives us a lot of business from the major industries here.

One such industry is the wedding venues on the strip. There are hundreds of chapels dotting the Las Vegas Boulevard, and all are trying to sell the same thing to the same audience.

A chapel retained our firm to help them increase

their web rankings. Like all of our clients, we started by looking through their website to analyze their ability to rank.

We always start with an assessment simply because sites that don't perform well with current traffic probably won't do any better with SEO.

We found that the site was using hundreds of plugins, most of which were outdated. The problem this posed was twofold.

First, with that many plugins each page took almost 30 seconds to load. In a world of impatient Internet users this is just unacceptable.

The second issue was the security threats from so many outdated plugins that had been neglected over the years. They were an open door to hackers.

The first thing we recommended was to remove the outdated plugins and consolidate any remaining into updated plugins with ongoing support.

Unfortunately, our business relationship ended since this particular business didn't take well to consultants who didn't agree with them.

I don't say this out of bitterness or resentment, but to make a point that if you have a business, treat it like a business. Make choices that will grow and keep it healthy.

If you treat your business like a spoiled child, your return will be about the same. If you're disciplined and do what's best for the business, even if it makes you a little uncomfortable, you will end up with a money producing machine that gives you the wealth you desired when starting it in the first place.

But I digress.

Unfortunately, this chapel ended up getting hacked through their plugins a couple of months later and all of their pages showed a warning that the site had been compromised. Not the best reputation to have online.

Since we don't keep tabs on former clients I don't know what they ended up doing to fix their site. I share this case study as a lesson to remember: plugins are important tools but must be maintained properly.

You don't have any reason to use outdated ones or any that don't benefit your site. It is always better to have a plain text page than a page with a fancy plugin that hurts your SEO with page speed issues. Play it safe and stick with healthy plugins that don't hurt your on-page SEO or user experience.

Things to Ponder

1. What plugins do you use on your site currently? What purpose do they serve?

2. Of the plugins on your site are there any that could be removed?

3. Are there any plugins uploaded to your site that are not active but still slowing the site down?

4. Of the plugins, how many users actually actively use the functions the plugins offer?

5. Of the plugins how many of them are essential to running your business and how many are just for fun?

6. What plugins are regularly updated by

developers? Which ones are getting older? Have any had security issues you are aware of?

End of Chapter Challenge

If you are not a developer, you should include one in this end of chapter challenge.

The idea is to figure out what plugins you need and don't need and also which ones are helping or hurting your site.

If you have a good developer, they may have already done this. If not don't worry; just work through these steps together.

First, make a complete backup of your website. You want to make sure if you break anything that you can easily revert the site back to how you had it.

Next copy the backup to a test URL so you can actively test the site and not worry about live users seeing the edits. If you don't have this option and want to do this exercise on your live site, make sure you have a working back up you can get quickly.

Next go to Google Page Speed Insights and type in your URL or the URL of the test domain you are working on.

Copy all the errors that come up onto a separate page so you can check them later against your new data.

Next, go to the plugins area of your website and deactivate all plugins regardless of what they are. This will most likely make your site look horrible but what we are doing is cleaning the code and taking it down to the bare bones.

Run the page speed insights again and see how many errors were removed.

Next remove all images that aren't optimized from the page you are testing so you can easily get rid of the image error.

Finally, go into your header.php file or the file that contains your header script and comment out the CSS and JavaScript files. What this will do is leave your page as basically text with no external loading resources.

Now, go to Page Speed Insights again and test the

page. You should get a 100% or close to it now that all the elements that cause errors have been removed.

The only issue now is that you have an ugly site (probably).

Now working backwards, start adding back in each element you removed to see how many errors are created.

The CSS can usually remain if you minify it with one of the online minify tools. The JavaScript is sometimes the same depending on how regularly it is updated and needs to be read on the site.

Optimize the images using the loss or lossless optimizer online and re-upload. This should allow the images to show without generating errors.

Lastly, activate one plugin at a time starting with the most important to see how many (if any) errors show up.

By following this process we have been able to increase our page speed to very high scores that had formerly been knocked down by plugins or tools that weren't well coded.

Citations

[1] Content Management Systems, Tuts+, https://code.tutsplus.com/articles/top-10-most-usable-content-management-systems--net-6493

[2] Google Page Speed Insights, Google, https://developers.google.com/speed/pagespeed/insights/

[3] Render Blocking Javascript Removal, Google Developers, https://developers.google.com/speed/docs/insights/BlockingJS

[4] Best Wordpress Cache Plugins, Shout Me Loud https://www.shoutmeloud.com/best-wordpress-cache-plugin-faster-loading-wp.html

Online Resources

Online resources for this chapter can be found at: https://josephstevenson.com/little-book-seo-part-1-on-page-ch7/

Links to citations, discussions and submission of additional resources by readers are available for each chapter.

To be notified of future books in the *Little Book on Digital Marketing Series* please email littlebook@josephstevenson.com or visit our website at http://josephstevenson.com/little-book/ and enter your email in the form provided.

Page Speed

Get It Fast

"Fast is fine, but accuracy is everything."

- Wyatt Earp

Why

It Really Matters

I have this infatuation with page speed optimization. Honestly, I don't really know why, but I think it has something to do with the technical aspects of SEO.

Page speed has always played a role in on-page SEO but with mobile users being at an all-time high [1], it matters more than ever.

I spoke with a client today who just checked his Google Analytics account and found that an astounding 71% of his users were on mobile devices while looking at his site.

The majority of his traffic comes from SEO, which makes his mobile optimization and speed a huge factor in his online strategy.

Google has a huge focus now on Page Speed [2] and websites that don't comply with the new way of doing things will most likely get penalized. There are some good reasons from Google for their crackdown on slow websites in their index. I am not going to go into that right now but instead want to focus on the main points behind why page speed matters to SEO.

People are Impatient

We haven't had to wait more than a few seconds since dial up modems became Internet history. Nowadays if you have a site load for more than a few seconds, it is normal to click back and find another site.

This could be due to the server your site is hosted on, but most likely it is an issue with your page that is causing the slow load speed.

You could write a blog post about how people need to be more patient, but I think you would be better off accepting that people are impatient and you have to deliver a fast site to keep their attention.

Speed = Less Bandwidth

Despite what people think, Google is not actually free. They have to pay quite a bit to keep their servers up and their crawlers moving. Websites that take up a lot of bandwidth will usually get crawled less. This makes sense in terms of resource allocation. But it doesn't help your slow site one bit.

Slow Sites Seem Outdated

Back to user experience, if you have a slow site most people will assume you are outdated and old. If that is what you are going for, then no worries, but most people want their website to be fast and new.

Usually a slowly loading site will bring up text first, followed by images, and then other media. This can make the site seem pretty ugly when only parts of it show up initially. A good rule of thumb is to try and have an up-to-date site if you plan to be competitive.

The Real Reason Why

The real reason you need to make sure your site has a good speed is because of the implications it has for your business.

Nobody should ever settle for less. If you've read this far and are still thinking, "Oh that doesn't sound so bad," you might want to re-think your motivation for having a website in the first place.

If you settle for less, that's exactly what you'll get -- and your competition will blow past you. If you are competing in the online space, there is literally no room for error and laziness on a business owner's part. It can equal huge losses with online sales, profitability, and brand image.

How

The Technical and Not So

Hopefully I have sufficiently impressed upon you the importance of page speed and how it can affect your site and user experience.

Now is the fun implementation part of the chapter where I get to show you how to increase your page speed and at the same time your user satisfaction level. I may repeat some of the concepts I put in previous chapters, but I won't go into as much detail.

Let's jump right in!

Server

Your server is the first place to start with page speed. You can use a tool like Bitcatcha [3] to figure out how fast your server is.

If you don't know what everything means on the pages don't worry I'll break down the basics.

MS: This represents the microseconds it takes for your site to load. The lower the number the faster your site will be.

Locations: There are different locations based on where your site is getting pinged. You don't want any false readings from a ping that is next door to the company that hosts your site.

IP: This is the server that hosts your site. It's helpful to know if you are worried about being on a spammed or blacklisted server. You can check the status of your IP using a tool like What is My IP Address [4] to see if you have a safe rating.

If your server has decent speed and reviews you can move on to the next step. If not, try looking for more a reputable website hosting service. You will probably have to pay more but you will end up with a much better experience in the long run. I prefer WP Engine [5] for hosting since they have amazing customer support, automatic backups, and all the core files are static so you don't have to worry as much about getting hacked.

I am not paid to endorse them; I just wanted to give them a mention because of my positive experience so far. You may have a similar experience with your own host.

Media

Once you have pinned down a good server it's time to look at the heaviest-to-load resources on your website, which is usually the media.

Using a tool like Google Page Speed Insights [6], check your domain for any images that need optimized. If you have a lot of errors, try removing the images from the page temporarily until you can get a better score.

Videos are best hosted on public servers like YouTube [7], or Vimeo [8]. If privacy is a concern you can opt to protect your videos and make them accessible only through your website.

Properly optimized media will usually jump your page speed up dramatically from any previous levels without the need to make a lot of further adjustments.

Code Order

Depending on what you have on your page, the order the code loads in could make a difference. If you use a lot of plugins or widgets, you may have issues with slow loading due to external scripts that need to load before more important content or applications. You can use the Google Page Speed Insights tool to check for this error, or disable your plugins and then check the page speed to quickly assess whether this is an issue.

It's better to have a developer take off plugins and rebuild them as customized into the site, instead of having too many external resources that slow your site down.

Ask yourself how important the plugin is to user experience, and if there isn't a huge need, take it out and improve your speed.

User Device

This is an area you can't control. If you are testing your site's page speed on a mobile device or network, make sure you work in a few tests on different devices.

Often people will assume that because their phone is slow at loading the website, that it's the website owners fault, when in reality it's the phone network's fault.

Again, there isn't a lot you can do about this, but knowing that it is an issue can save you a lot of time and money when working on page speed.

Summary

Don't be afraid to take down and build back up your site in an effort to make it as fast as possible. Many users have left websites before making a purchase due to slow user experience.

Don't let a slow website affect your chances of making a sale or improving your rankings!

Case Study

Celebrity Blog

I have had the opportunity to help a few celebrity bloggers increase their page speed. The problem has always been the same; usually having to do with millions of users hitting their site, with only a handful of them staying due to slow page load speed.

This often translated into thousands of dollars in lost revenue per day, which of course was unacceptable for any of these clients.

The common factor I found on each of these sites was that they were on a slow server that couldn't handle the needs of their growing blog, and their code was outdated, making the content difficult for the user to load.

The most difficult site was a Mommy blog that was getting around a million hits per day. After doing some analysis we noticed that she was only getting about half of the reported traffic to stay and read her posts.

With a bounce rate of 50% we knew something had to be wrong, especially since the titles of the posts matched the topic exactly.

We quickly discovered that half the users were getting time-out errors on her site due to the server having a slow load speed. She was losing about $500 per day in ad revenue from these lost users and was at a pretty desperate point when we consulted with her on some new server recommendations.

After some chatting we decided as a team to get her site migrated over to an Amazon Web Server [9]. We set up a new instance and partitioned off different sections of the server to handle different load amounts. The idea was that if too much traffic hit at one point, the server would balance the traffic over multiple instances and be able to handle the load.

Immediately with some tests we found that the site could handle around 10,000 hits per minute without any lag time, which was more than enough to handle her traffic.

The results from her side were nothing short of spectacular. Her daily revenue from ads more than doubled and her user retention went way up increasing her sales even more.

I can't take credit for this huge success only because it was a huge win to use Amazon as our hosting server. Although it was difficult to configure, it ended up being incredibly worthwhile for her in the long run to do the migration.

We did have to make a few additional code changes to her site in order to make sure her page speed was up to par, but once we migrated, it fixed about 90% of her load speed issues.

Things to Ponder

1. How fast is your website? Without doing any tests, load your website. How does it feel? If it weren't your site, would you stick around?

2. What plugins do you use on your site? Do they slow it down? How essential are they to user experience?

3. Of your competitors, are their websites faster or slower than yours? Use a Who is hosting tool to see where your competitors host their website. Are they paying more or less for hosting than you?

4. Of the competitors that are faster than you, how many of them rank higher in search engines? Do you think their page speed correlates with their rankings?

5. Have a developer look at your site. Do they

have recommendations for page speed adjustments? How close are their assessments to Google's Page Speed Insights?

6. Are there external resources loading on your site that slow it down? Are these necessary? How much would it affect you to remove them from your site in order to increase your page speed?

End of Chapter Challenge

I love the end of chapter challenges since it's my turn to test your knowledge from the chapter and also uncover how your website is doing with the principle that was taught.

With this being a speed chapter, you may want to include your developer in on this test to figure out together how you fare.

Make sure you do a backup of your site and work offline to increase page speed.

First, go to Google Page Speed Insights and test your site. Write the score below:

Score: ______________________________

Next: Analyze the speed errors (if any) on the page. If you don't have any errors; then amazing! Skip to the next chapter.

You can analyze these by clicking the down-arrow next to each error description. This will load the files or resources that are causing slow loading of your site.

Once you can see what your main errors are, write them below:

____

____

____

____

____

____

____

____

____

Now that you have the error recorded, do the following to see how many can be removed:

1. Remove all images from the page you are testing.

2. Go to the header and footer files and remove the JavaScript and CSS resources. Preferably just comment them out since you will need them later.

3. Disable all plugins and external tools on the site.

Now go back and re-check for errors and write them below:

____

____

____

____

____

____

____

____

If done correctly you should have very few if no errors. Now you can go backwards and re-add pictures and the elements to your pages including the plugins.

Test your page speed as you go for any errors that come back so you can easily determine which ones are causing issues.

Once you have finished re-enabling all of your plugins and added back all of your media do a full test to see if your overall score has improved. If not you probably haven't fixed anything. If you have; then, congratulations, you just optimized your site for page speed!

Citations

[1] Smart Inishgts, Mobile Marketing Stistics Compilation, http://www.smartinsights.com/mobile-marketing/mobile-marketing-analytics/mobile-marketing-statistics/

[2] Google, PageSpeed Insights Rules, https://developers.google.com/speed/docs/insights/rules

[3] Bitcatcha, How Fast is Your Hosting, https://www.bitcatcha.com/

[4] What is My IP Address, Blacklist Check, http://whatismyipaddress.com/blacklist-check

[5] WP Engine, Dedicated Wordpress Hosting, https://wpengine.com

[6] Google Page Speed Insights, https://developers.google.com/speed/pagespeed/insights/

[7] Youtube, https://youtube.com

[8] Vimeo, https://vimeo.com

[9] Amazon Web Server, https://aws.amazon.com

Online Resources

Online resources for this chapter can be found at:

https://josephstevenson.com/little-book-seo-part-1-on-page-ch8/

Links to citations, discussions and submission of additional resources by readers are available for each chapter.

To be notified of future books in the *Little Book on Digital Marketing Series* please email littlebook@josephstevenson.com or visit our website at http://josephstevenson.com/little-book/ and enter your email in the form provided.

Mobile Optimization

More Traffic Potential

"Life... It tends to respond to our outlook, to shape itself to meet our expectations."

- Richard M. DeVos

Why

Mobile is More Important than Desktop

A couple of years ago Google announced that they would be making changes to their search algorithm by putting an emphasis on sites that have a solid mobile version.

At that point, a lot of sites had already adopted either a dedicated mobile site or a responsive website [1]. Some however still only had desktop versions making them difficult to view on mobile devices.

Google is all about user experience, so it was inevitable with the rise of mobile Internet usage that websites would have to conform.

Initially Google did a roll out around April 21st of 2015 [2], but since then they have made continual updates to the mobile algorithm including separating the desktop and mobile versions [3], and adding Accelerated Mobile Pages or AMP [4].

With every update, websites that have built mobile versions of their content have been rewarded and sites that have stuck with their desktop versions have seen declines in rankings.

With the introduction of different desktop and mobile crawlers, Google put emphasis on the mobile version due to the mass volume of users they have on those devices.

Whether you are with the mobile revolution or not, if you don't have a good solid mobile version of your website, you aren't going to do well with SEO.

Speed is a Factor

Mobile sites are particularly affected by server speed and clean code.

Many websites that have mobile versions don't see any ranking improvements due to their mobile version being slow to load.

Even if you have the most beautiful mobile website, if you can't be accessed in less than a couple of seconds, users will just click the back button, and Google will penalize you for page speed and bounce rate.

If you have speed issues still, I would go back and review the previous chapters to see how you can improve your website.

Remember that some users will be accessing your website using smartphones on networks that aren't that great. You need to make sure that you have the best version of your site as possible on the web to get in front of all users, even those who have slow connections.

Getting to It

Like some of the other chapters, this one will have some technical advice. I would suggest you talk with your developer or have them look through the chapter, then check your website for compliance.

As always make sure you have a solid backup of your site before you do any edits or changes to the live version. When creating responsive themes or dedicated mobile sites you will need to change the core files which could potentially affect your current site.

Always play it safe and have a solid backup plan if things go horribly wrong.

How

Getting to Mobile Compliance

Knowing you need a mobile compliant site is just a small part of the battle. If you don't currently have a mobile compliant site, you will have to build one.

If you do have one you will still want to check and see how Google views your site.

Before proceeding go to Google's Mobile Friendly Test [5] and enter your URL.

Much like the Google Page Speed Insights Tool [6], the Mobile Friendly Test will analyze your site to check for compliance with their mobile search algorithm.

Once you know where you stand you can decide if you need to build a new mobile version, or edit what you currently have.

I will discuss both and my opinion on the pros and cons of each. You will need a developer or have some programming knowledge to make these changes. Since this is a book about on-page optimization and not coding, I will go into what needs to happen, but not the in-depth code explanations.

Dedicated Mobile

Dedicated mode is having a completely separate site for your mobile version. Usually you have a script in your .htaccess file that will forward your users based on the screen size of the device they are using [7].

The major benefits of having a dedicated mobile site are also seen as some of the major cons for responsive fans. Although I generally stick with responsive web design, I will try to remain objective when reviewing both.

As I mentioned, with dedicated you are able to have separate code completely for your mobile site. This makes it easy to remove and show content to mobile users differently than you would for desktop users.

Often, I will have clients that want to mainly show phone numbers and addresses on their mobile sites since their users are usually looking for directions. Having a dedicated site makes this really simple since you can code the content directly.

A downside of doing the coding this way is that you take up more search engine resources. Now search engines have to crawl your site twice to access the same data. Additionally, you have to decide if you want users to see the mobile version for their iPads or other smaller screens.

It can be very difficult to pick a version when users may have a larger screen, but it is still considered a mobile device.

One other con is that you have to update your content twice whenever there is a change.

Some may not see this is a big deal, but if you have a site that requires new content often it will become a pain to update both versions every time you have a change.

Responsive

Like I mentioned before, responsive design has some of the benefits that dedicated users would see as a con.

With responsive, you have just one website for

both the desktop and mobile version. The CSS code on your site reacts based on the screen size of the user's device.

Much like how you redirect users in the .htaccess file on the dedicated side, with responsive you show different styling based on the screen size in the CSS file.

The benefit of this is that you can have a nice-looking site that changes as you resize the window in your browser. Regardless of the screen size of current or future devices, you will have a nice-looking site.

The cons are that it is much more difficult to build a responsive site than a dedicated mobile one. Responsive sites have to change and morph as you resize the screen, which makes it challenging for some developers to display all of your content in a way that is visually impressive on all devices.

This can add a lot of time and effort to projects (not to mention headaches) if you have some specific tastes that require all versions of your sites.

Another problem is that many sites that have had

mobile versions already don't want to deal with the hassle of forwarding over their mobile versions to their new responsive desktop versions.

Older sites that have thousands of pages indexed would need to have an extensive redirect plan in place before launching the new site in order to make sure they don't lose any rankings they currently have.

The biggest pro for a responsive site is that you have one site and one code that translates across all devices. This makes crawling your website easy for search engines, and if a new device comes out that has an odd screen size, you will be covered before dedicated sites.

Case Study

Pest Management

We have a client who uses us for custom coding and other tedious projects. When we first met they had a separate mobile site and desktop site.

They had employed developers in the past to launch a new responsive site, but had never been able to get a functioning version.

When we were hired, it was to only create a site that was responsive in hopes that their SEO would improve.

Much like any other mobile version, they had large buttons and less content on the mobile pages versus the desktop pages. This was a strategy put in place to help with user friendliness and experience. The content still matched the main site, but there was just much less of it.

Our first goal was to update all the code so it would be responsive before we removed the mobile version. The hope was that when we launched the responsive version, we would be able to do so without anyone noticing and then just redirect the old site over to the new responsive one.

The site itself had a lot of outdated code like Flash [8] and Tables [9] that generally don't do well on mobile versions.

After going page by page removing tables and adding in some divs, we had to make each one respond to screen the various screen sizes on all devices.

We started by removing all set width on elements and instead set them to a percent of the screen they used like 100% for full width pages, and 30/70% for pages with sidebars.

As the screens sized down we would use the @Media Function [10] to change the element percent to match what would better fit on the page.

Generally, we would make the pages with sidebars go from 30/70% to 50/50% and then 100%. As the screen sized down, we switched the content to 50/50 on the iPad versions and then 100% stacking on top of each other for phones.

We made these changes throughout the entire site, removing tables and Flash and updating all the shortocdes with the right classes or ids to match the new responsive design.

The Result

I actually just had a call with the owner a couple of days ago and he was happy to report that their site score had reached in the high 30's for MOZ.

He went on to relay that until we had made those changes, they had never been able to get their site score above 20.

This was a huge indicator of our success, not to mention the Google Analytics data increase on the mobile side, to 70% of all users.

With these combined we called this project a very big success. We are still working to optimize any old archived and indexed content, but the last time we checked, the site was seeing double the online traffic and leads.

Things to Ponder

1. Do you have a mobile site? Is it easy or difficult to use? What content is on your mobile site that is not on your desktop? What content is on your desktop that is not on your mobile?

2. How fast does the mobile version of your site load? Have you tested it in multiple locations? What about with and without Wi-Fi?

3. What would you change about your mobile site if anything?

4. What is the purpose of the mobile version of your site versus the desktop version? If the purpose is the same, do you have the same content and call to actions on both versions of the site?

End of Chapter Challenge

This end of chapter challenge will be hopefully educational but also useful in determining how your site is doing with mobile or responsive design.

If you aren't comfortable with coding make sure you have your developer sit on in this one so you can both make sure you are doing things right.

First Go to Google's Mobile Friendly Test and check your site. Enter the results below:

If you have a passing grade try entering a friend

or colleagues site until you find one that needs some help.

Next analyze what the site is doing on the mobile version. Determine if they are missing a mobile version or if their mobile version isn't functioning correctly. Test by sizing down the site on your browser or by loading the site on your mobile device. Describe below what you see:

____

____

____

____

____

List the major problem points you see with the mobile version. Look for things like the text being too small to read without zooming in, or images that are off the screen. Remember proper mobile versions should be easy to read without zooming or waiting for long loading resources. List the problems below:

____

____

____

____

Are the problems site-wide or page specific? If the issue were the text being too small on all the pages it would need to be fixed site-wide. On the other hand, if you find that another page loads nicely then it is probably page specific.

List your answer below:

Using your answers, you should now have a plan to create or fix the mobile version of your site, or the one you're analyzing.

The basics you need to know are:

1. If your site is mobile friendly.

2. What mobile improvements are needed to make the site compliant?

3. What code changes you need that will make the improvements live.

Using the following page formulate a plan with your developer to make the site mobile friendly. This does not need to be an extremely technical plan, but instead can focus on the problem areas you see, and what needs to happen to make your site compliant.

Use Google Page Speed Test or Mobile Friendly test to help you spot problem areas.

Citations

[1] Responsive Vs Mobile Sites, All Web Codesign, http://allwebcodesign.com/responsive-vs-mobile-sub.htm

[2] Google's Mobile Friendly Update, MOZ, https://moz.com/blog/9-things-about-googles-mobile-friendly-update

[3] Google is Splitting its Search Index, Prioritizing Mobile over Desktop, https://www.searchenginejournal.com/google-splitting-search-index-prioritizing-mobile-desktop/176149/

[4] Accelerated Mobile Pages, AMP, AMP Project, https://www.ampproject.org/

[5] Google's Mobile Friendly Test, https://search.google.com/test/mobile-friendly

[6] Google Page Speed Insights, https://developers.google.com/speed/pagespeed/insights/

[7] How to Redirect Your Website to its Mobile Version, http://www.inmotionhosting.com/support/website/redirects/mobile-redirect

[8] Adobe Flash, https://en.wikipedia.org/wiki/Adobe_Flash

[9] HTML Tables, W3C Schools, https://www.w3schools.com/html/html_tables.asp

[10] CSS3 @Media Rule, https://www.w3schools.com/cssref/css3_pr_mediaquery.asp

[11] Google Analytics, https://analytics/google.com/

Online Resources

Online resources for this chapter can be found at:

https://josephstevenson.com/little-book-seo-part-1-on-page-ch9/

Links to citations, discussions and submission of additional resources by readers are available for each chapter.

To be notified of future books in the *Little Book on Digital Marketing Series* please email littlebook@josephstevenson.com or visit our website at http://josephstevenson.com/little-book/ and enter your email in the form provided.

10

Schema and Tags

"It's the little things that kill."

- Gavin Rossdale

Why

What they are

Tagging content is like an extra layer of identification for search engines when they're crawling your content.

Think about an address. In the U.S., you have the first line, which is usually a building number followed by street name, type of street and unit number. The next line is the city, state, and zip code.

If you are from the U.S. and have a basic education, reading and address is simple.

However, if you are a search engine, reading content on a page with code and plain text, it can be a little more difficult.

89101 is a zip code in downtown Las Vegas. I know if I see a line that says "Las Vegas, NV 89101" then I am looking at an address.

Search engines however could be looking at anything and have to index the content the best way they know how.

Using tagging or schema markups you can identify certain types of content. From the folks over at Schema.org [1], here is a rough summary:

Schema.org is a collaborative, community activity with a mission to create, maintain, and promote schemas for structured data on the Internet, on web pages, in email messages, and beyond.

Schema.org vocabulary can be used with many different encodings, including RDFa, Microdata and JSON-LD. These vocabularies cover entities, relationships between entities and actions, and can easily be extended through a well-documented extension model. Over 10 million sites use Schema.org to mark-up their web pages and email messages. Many applications from Google, Microsoft, Pinterest, Yandex and others already use these vocabularies to power rich, extensible experiences.

Founded by Google, Microsoft, Yahoo and Yandex, Schema.org vocabularies are developed by an open community process, using the public-schemaorg@w3.org mailing list [2] and through Github [3].

A shared vocabulary makes it easier for webmasters and developers to decide on a schema and get the maximum benefit for their efforts. It is in this spirit that the founders, together with the larger community have come together - to provide a shared collection of schemas.

In a nutshell, your content needs to be wrapped with tags just like html does to style your content.

The tags will tell search engines what type of content you have on your page so it can be properly indexed.

To add the markup to your site you will want to research on schema.org but as a quick lesson I will include some code snippets that explain the basics.

Before We Start Our Last Lesson

This is the last chapter before we go into resources. If you are looking for more help you can always reach out to us at our firm by emailing littlebook@josephstevenson.com.

Additionally, you can check out Google Webmasters [4] and look through their various resources to see if your site is optimized.

You will be able to find information on schema, keywords, health, page speed, and more with this free tool.

How

Adding Schema and Tags to Your Site

There are a few ways to add tags to your site using plugins or hard coding it directly into your content.

I am going to give you the exact code to use so that whether you are going with a plugin or html, you will know what is going on with your content.

Item Properties

To start with, there are different vocabularies to know when you are working with schema tags. The "itemprop" is one of the most used identifiers and should be a big part of your process.

Going back to the address example again, I will show you the before and after of what an address looks like to search engines with and without the markup.

Here is the example:

Your Business Name
Contact Details:

Main Address:

123 S. Las Vegas BLVD
Las Vegas, NV 89101

Telephone:
(702) 123-4567

As I mentioned before, search engines will read this as text only and index it the best way they can.

Most will see it as a local address, but others may not be depending on how your data is crawled.

Now with the markup added:

```
<div itemscope
itemtype="http://schema.org/Organization">

<span itemprop="name">Your Business
Name</span>

Contact Details:

<div itemprop="address" itemscope
itemtype="http://schema.org/PostalAddress">

Main address:

<span itemprop="streetAddress">123 S Las Vegas
BLVD</span>
```

```
<span itemprop="postalCode">89101</span>

<span itemprop="addressLocality">Las Vegas,
NV</span>

</div>

Telephone:

<span itemprop="telephone">(702) 123-
4567</span>

</div>
```

Whether you are a programmer or not, you should be able to see the address buried within the code.

If you look closely you can see that the entire code is wrapped in a link tag back to the schema.org organization page. This tells search engines what type of data the entire block is.

Next there are individual item properties wrapped around different content.

In order, you have:

Name
Address
Street Address
Postal Code

Address Locality
Telephone

These tags have the content embedded in each

one corresponding with the correct itemprop.

Now when the content is crawled, each piece is recognized and stored according to type making it much more useful to major search engines.

There are literally hundreds of different markup styles to choose from based on the content you have on your page.

We could write an entire book just on schema markup. It's likely there is already one out there.

To begin with, start with your most basic site data that is repeated on each page and mark it up.

This could be the copyright text in your footer, the address or phone number in your menu bar, or images you use for your logos throughout the site.

Once you have marked up a few pieces of content, it gets exponentially easier to do for all of your content.

Case Study

Las Vegas SEO

When schema.org first came out I had only been focusing on content in the traditional sense, which was adding in location keywords to my main targets.

This worked fine at the time since it was the norm, but when I discovered schema.org I was able to take my coding to the next level.

At the time, although I was only targeting Las Vegas, I didn't have any special markup to tell search engines what my geographic location was or where I preferred to target.

When I started, I didn't know anything about schema so I downloaded the local plugin from Yoast [5] and let the auto fill settings do the work.

I immediately saw an improvement in my local rankings and it correlated perfectly with my schema integration.

Since then, I have manually adjusted my content to match each schema type as I enter it in.

You can auto add tags around your future content by adjusting your theme templates to have schema tags around certain properties like your header elements or descriptions.

The same is true for hundreds of other content types that schema can markup. For a full list see the Microdata [6] section of schema.org.

Once I started adding in tags based on content type, I saw my rankings and traffic increase substantially. My users were more accurate and looking for what I was selling, and as a result, my conversion rate when through the roof.

A True Principle with Anything

Am I saying if you add schema.org tags to your site that immediately you will rank better? No.

Am I saying that if you don't add it you will see your rankings tank and your business go up in flames? Of course not.

This book is meant to give you the most basic On-Page SEO tools you need to successfully optimize your page according to current best practice web standards.

If you aren't currently following them, most likely not implementing will not do much to your current rankings.

If you do add them, usually the additions will only bring improvements to your rankings and SEO.

Things to Ponder

1. What content do you have on your site that might only be recognizable to you but not machines?

2. Does the content on your site have enough explanations to give search engines an idea about your business?

3. If you stripped all of the keywords from your content what would your site be about? Would search engines know where you are or what you sell without them?

4. Of all the content on your site, what is in most need of markup? What is the most important thing you need customers or users to see when they are visiting your site? Is that content front and center for them and for search engines?

5. What if anything is misleading about your content whether unintentionally or intentionally?

End of Chapter Challenge

To get your site geared up for schema.org I am going to assume you don't have any tags and jump right into the challenge.

If you do have everything implemented then you probably aren't reading this chapter anyway.

First go to your contact page and find the address. If you don't have an address find the contact page that has your phone number or email.

If you don't have any of these I would suggest just creating one for test purposes and then deleting it later if you have specific reasons why you don't want people having your contact information for your business.

Next, take the code that was used previously and add your content where the all capitalized content is below:

```
<div itemscope
itemtype="http://schema.org/Organization">

<span itemprop="name">Your Business
Name</span>
```

Contact Details:

```
<div itemprop="address" itemscope
itemtype="http://schema.org/PostalAddress">

<span itemprop="streetAddress">STREET
ADDRESS</span>

<span itemprop="postalCode">ZIP CODE</span>

<span itemprop="addressLocality">CITY,
STATE</span>

</div>
```

Telephone:

```
<span itemprop="telephone">PHONE
NUMBER</span>

</div>
```

Now take the completed code and copy it back into the text version of your contact page.

It's important to put it in the text version or you will end up with formatted code to be read by users and not computers.

Once you have saved it, take a look on the front end and make sure the address is still readable to human eyes.

Then right click on the page and view the source code to make sure the address is wrapped how you want it according to schema.org standards.

Last of all go to Google Webmaster tools and re-submit your site for crawling. After a few days you should be able to see markup in the proper sections for your first bit of marked up code.

Citations

[1] Schema.org, https://schema.org

[2] W3.org, https://w3.org

[3] Github, https://github.com

[4] Google Webmaster Tools, https://webmasters.google.com

[5] Yoast, https://yoast.com

[6] Schema.org, Microdata, http://schema.org/docs/gs.html

Online Resources

Online resources for this chapter can be found at: https://josephstevenson.com/little-book-seo-part-1-on-page-ch10/

Links to citations, discussions and submission of additional resources by readers are available for each chapter.

To be notified of future books in the *Little Book on Digital Marketing Series* please email littlebook@josephstevenson.com or visit our website at http://josephstevenson.com/little-book/ and enter your email in the form provided.

11

Resources

My On-Page Optimization Tools

Throughout this book I have referenced a lot of the tools I use. I wanted to create a comprehensive resource with instructions on the best ways to use these tools for on-page SEO.

I am not endorsing or getting paid to promote any of these tools or websites.

I will be putting a page on my website with some of the resources you found in this book. Please visit:

https://josephstevenson.com/little-book-seo-part-1-on-page-resources/

If you have any resources for on-page optimization, please feel free to add them in the comments section of that page online.

To be notified of future books in the *Little Book on Digital Marketing Series*, please email littlebook@josephstevenson.com or visit our website at http://josephstevenson.com/little-book/ and enter your email in the form provided.

Yoast. I use the Yoast plugin to check the on-page optimization for all of my clients who use Wordpress as their CMS. Their tools do a decent job checking page content and generally helping to weed out any keyword injections or spam you might accidentally add during marketing.

All in One SEO Pack. This is a plugin much like Yoast and is used by about 50% of the market as far as I can tell. (Don't quote me on that number in case I'm wrong and someone shows up on my door with an angry face.) They do a great job as well, and deserve a mention.

Ahrefs. I use this tool to tell me a lot about off-site optimization. I also use it to help me with indexed to figure out the main keywords that I am showing up for. I highly recommend them if you are looking for a solid tool to analyze your site from a third-party perspective.

Alexa. This tool comes from some of my old school bag of resources and is still really helpful to determine the health and traffic of a site.

Spyfu. This is primarily a keyword research tool to spy on competitors. I have found it useful in tracking competitor sites to determine how they're using on-page optimization.

MOZ. I use MOZ to tell me a lot about the health of a website and especially any errors they find in the code. They are really helpful in pointing out on-page issues found while crawling and their blog always has awesome insight as well.

Google Webmaster Tools. I mention this a few times in the book. Google Webmaster Tools are really helpful to get a bird's eye view of how Google sees your site. In my opinion, it's imperative to track any potential threats to your site, including harmful backlinks.

Google Page Speed Insights. I use this tool almost daily to track the load speed of my client's sites and mine. It's another Google freebie and a lifesaver.

Search Engine Watch. I follow the people over there since they keep up pretty well on what is happening with search engines. Add them to your feed or subscribe to see any new on-page tactics Google is coming out with.

Search Engine Journal. Like Search Engine Watch, it's another goodie I use on a regular basis to stay sharp.

Hubspot. These guys offer paid services but they have a lot of free tools that help a ton when it comes to on-page SEO. Additionally, they have some lead gen tools that are pretty mind blowing.

Backlinko. I follow the news from these people since they tend to have new ideas I don't see a lot of other places. It's definitely worth the time to check out. They also cover some pretty interesting topics related to off-page optimization.

If I've missed any, don't forget to add them at https://josephstevenson.com/little-book-seo-part-1-on-page-resources/.

12

Conclusion

More Good Things to Come

I hope this book can be your roadmap for on-page optimization. Some of you reading this may be just learning digital marketing, while others may be seasoned, experienced marketers.

No matter where you are in your education, I hope you were able to find something useful from my experiences and stories.

If there are any faults in this book they are purely accidental. I hope the entire book won't be judged based on one or two items that change or become outdated with time.

As I mentioned, I have pages online dedicated to each chapter of the book. My hope is that those reading this book can feel a sense of ownership and share their experiences through comments on the pages found through my website.

Feel free to comment and share your opinions related to completing the exercises. I will publish all opinions as long as they are not trolling or harassing in nature.

This is the first in a series; I hope to cover digital marketing topics in short book format for every major topic.

If you would like to be notified of new books as they come out, please email littlebook@josephstevenson.com or go to josephstevenson.com and sign up for the mailing list.

Thank you so much for reading and I wish you the best of luck in your on-page optimization.

About the Author

Joseph Stevenson is an SEO Consultant, author and public speaker. He has more than 17 years of experience in digital marketing and is the CEO of Joseph Stevenson SEO, a Nevada-based firm.

83635862R00114

Made in the USA
Lexington, KY
14 March 2018